Visit www.PianoTab.com

Check out our other books & rate us at Amazon.com

to receive a FREE piano tab song when you

Contact us on our website.

How to Read Piano Tab

This method of piano tab takes the note symbols out of sheet music and replaces them with letters.

- You read letters starting at the top and moving to the bottom of the page.

- A keyboard template is used as a guide, visible at the top of each page.

- Middle "C" is colored red or blue in the keyboard template header for easy reference on where to start the song.

- The rhythm count or beat is located in the left column along with each measure number and chords if needed.

- Notes played with the left hand are colored blue.

- Notes played with the right hand are colored red.

- As needed, fingering numbers are next to the note letters.

- When 2 or more notes are written horizontally, they are played together, indicated by a dotted line.

- A blue or red bold vertical line under a note letter represents a sustained count.

- A black "X" under a note letter represents a rest or staccato note.

Contents

River Flows In You
Yiruma

Key: A Major
BPM: 65

Piano Tab by Joe Caligiuri

Left Hand — Intro — Right Hand

Measure / Chord / Count / Hand

Free Flowing

Measure	Chord	Notes

Measure 1 — F#m / D

Count 1: F#, A⁵
Count &: C#², G#⁴
Count 2: F#¹, A
Count &: G#
Count 3: D⁵, A⁵
Count &: A², E²
Count 4: E¹, A⁵
Count &: D², A

Measure 2

Count &: A¹
Count a: C#²

Measure 3 — F#m / D

Count 1: F#, A⁵
Count &: C#², G#⁴
Count 2: F#¹, A⁵
Count &: G#⁴
Count 3: D⁵, A⁵
Count &: A², E²
Count 4: E¹, A⁵
Count &: D²

Measure 4

Count &: A¹
Count a: C#²

1

River Flows In You

Yiruma

Part 1

Left Hand   Right Hand

Piano Tab by
Joe Caligiuri

River Flows In You
Yiruma

Piano Tab by Joe Caligiuri

Key: A Major
BPM: 65

Left Hand · Part 1 · Right Hand

River Flows In You
Yiruma

Left Hand   *Part 1*   *Right Hand*

Piano Tab by
Joe Caligiuri

Key: A Major
BPM: 65

River Flows In You
Yiruma

River Flows In You

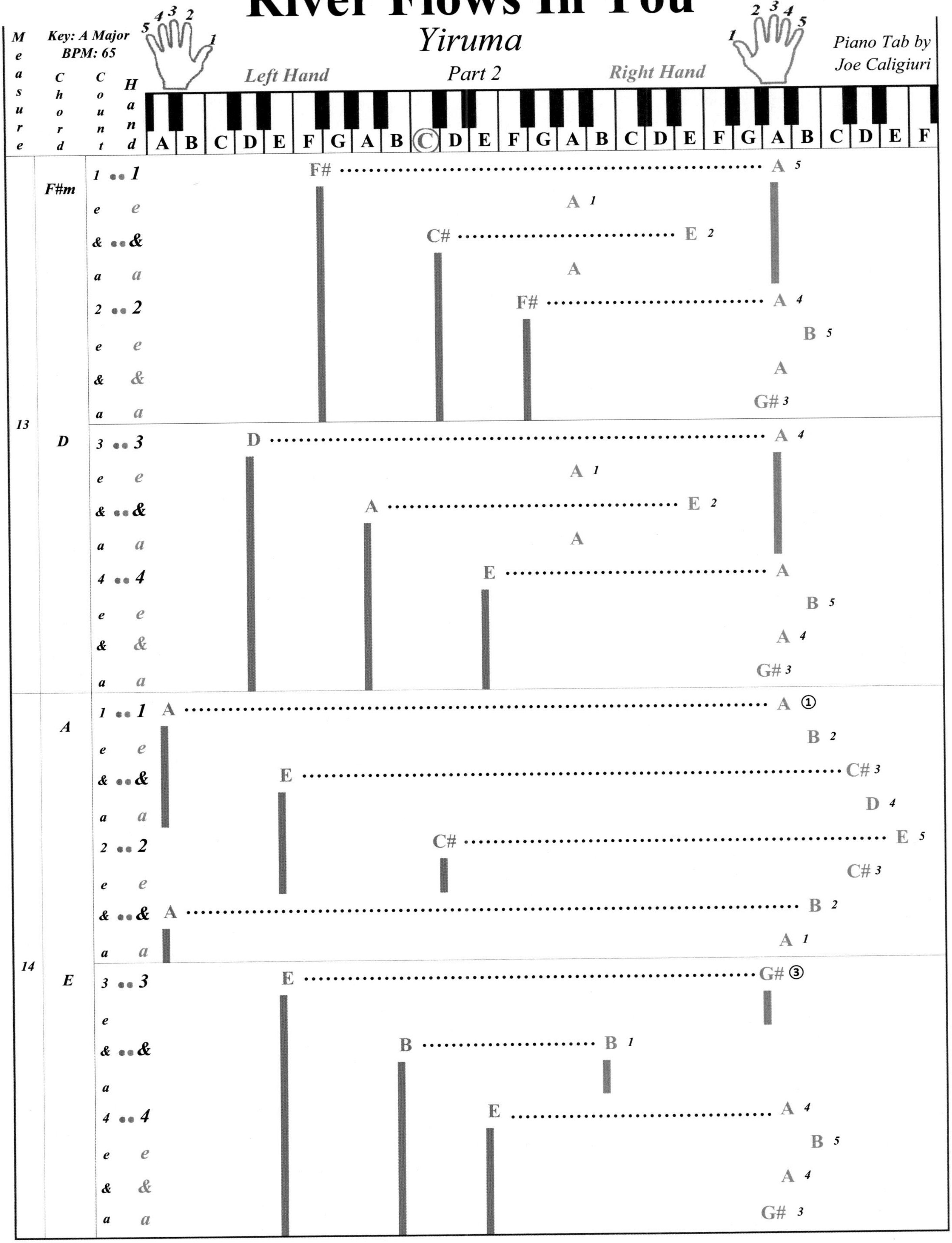

River Flows In You
Yiruma

Key: A Major
BPM: 65

Left Hand — Right Hand

Piano Tab by Joe Caligiuri

River Flows In You
Yiruma

Left Hand   Part 2   *Right Hand*

*Piano Tab by
Joe Caligiuri*

River Flows In You

Yiruma

Part 2

*Piano Tab by
Joe Caligiuri*

River Flows In You
Yiruma

Part 3

Piano Tab by
Joe Caligiuri

Left Hand   *Right Hand*

Key: A Major
BPM: 65

10

River Flows In You
Yiruma

Piano Tab by
Joe Caligiuri

Key: A Major
BPM: 65

Left Hand   Part 3   *Right Hand*

River Flows In You

Yiruma

Key: A Major
BPM: 65

Left Hand   Part 3   Right Hand

13

River Flows In You

Yiruma

Left Hand   *Part 3*   *Right Hand*

Piano Tab by
Joe Caligiuri

River Flows In You

Yiruma

Part 3

Piano Tab by Joe Caligiuri

15

River Flows In You

Yiruma

Piano Tab by
Joe Caligiuri

Left Hand — *Part 3* — *Right Hand*

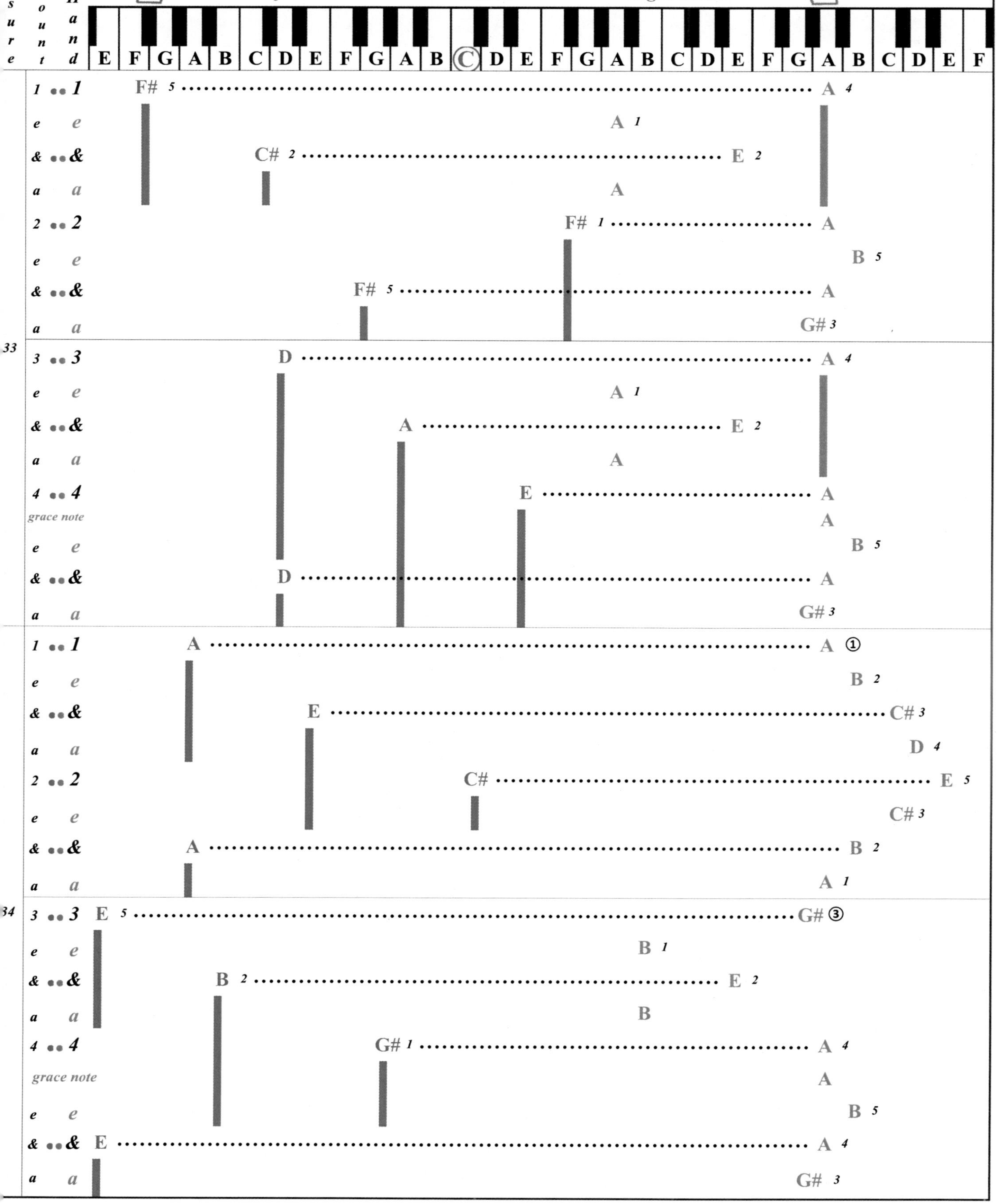

River Flows In You
Yiruma

Left Hand   *Part 3*   *Right Hand*

Piano Tab by Joe Caligiuri

River Flows In You
Yiruma
Part 4 - Outro

Left Hand   Right Hand

Piano Tab by Joe Caligiuri

River Flows In You
Yiruma
Part 4 - Outro

Piano Tab by
Joe Caligiuri

River Flows In You
Yiruma

Piano Tab by
Joe Caligiuri

Left Hand   Part 4 - Outro   *Right Hand*

River Flows In You

Yiruma

Left Hand   Part 4 - Outro   **Right Hand**

Piano Tab by Joe Caligiuri

Slow down tempo

Hold

21

Measures and Bar Lines

Measure	Count	Hand		

Left Hand   Right Hand

C D E F G A B C D E F G A B C D E F G A B C D E F G

Measure 1 — Count 1 2 3 4

A **bar line** divides music into **measures** (also called bars).

Breaking up the musical paragraph into smaller, measurable groups of notes.

Measure 2 — Count 1 2 3 4

Each **measure** has a specific number of beats - most commonly, four beats.

This sample Piano Tab sheet has 8 measures with four beats per measure.

Measure 3 — Count 1 2 3 4

Reading Piano Tab

Measure 4 — Count 1 2 3 4 / Hand 1

C 3

Left Hand Plays the C Below Middle C with Finger 3

Hold note 4 Beats (Whole Note)

Measure 5 — Count 1 2 3 4 / Hand 1

Right Hand Plays Middle C with Finger 1   C 1

Hold note 4 Beats (Whole Note)

Measure 6 — Count 1 2 3 4 / Hand 1

C 3 ·················· C 1

Dotted line indicates notes played together

Measure 7 — Count 1 2 3 4 / Hand 1 2 3 4

Hold C - 2 Beats C 3 ·················· C 1 Finger 1 (Quarter Note)

(Half Note) D 2 Finger 2 (Quarter Note)

Hold E - 2 Beats E 1 ·················· E 3 Finger 3 (Quarter Note)

(Half Note) F 4 Finger 4 (Quarter Note)

Measure 8 — Count 1 2 3 4 / Hand 1 2 3 4

C 3 ·················· C 1 (Two C's Played Together)

(2 Notes with Right Hand) D 2 ······ G 5 D & G Play Together

E 1 ·················· E 3 (Two E's Played Together)

F 4 (Only F Played)

22

The Keyboard and Middle C

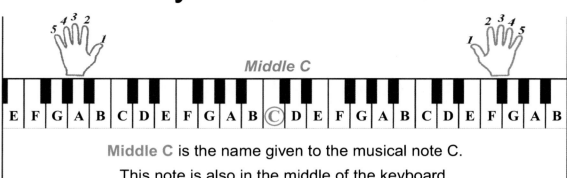

Middle C is the name given to the musical note C.
This note is also in the middle of the keyboard.

It's not actually quite in the middle of the keyboard,
but very close, and of all the C's on the piano
it is the one nearest to the middle.

On the piano or keyboard the Middle C is also known as C4.

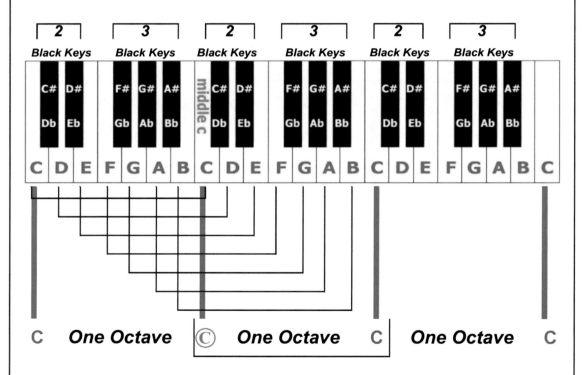

In an 88 key piano, there are 36 black keys and 52 white keys.

61 key keyboards come with 25 black keys and 36 white keys.

Sharps and Flats

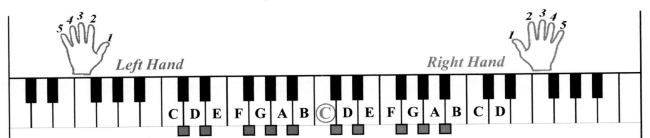

Sharps and flats are added after a note, for example C# or Db.

(I use a lower case b as a flat, it's roughly how it looks)

Putting a sharp symbol after a note, such as C
indicates the note is sharper, or higher pitched.
So C# is higher than C.

Putting a flat symbol after a musical letter tells you
it's lower, so for example Db is lower than D.
Also, sharps are often used going up,
and flats are used coming down the scale,
but this isn't a hard and fast rule.

Below I've listed the musical alphabet including sharps and flats, starting with a C.

Sharps: C C# D D# E F F# G G# A A# B C

Flats: C Db D Eb E F Gb G Ab A Bb B C

Notice there's no sharp or flats between <u>E and F</u>, nor between <u>B and C</u>.

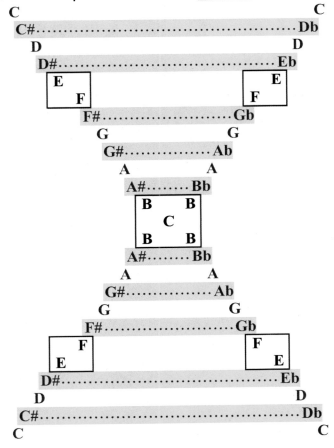

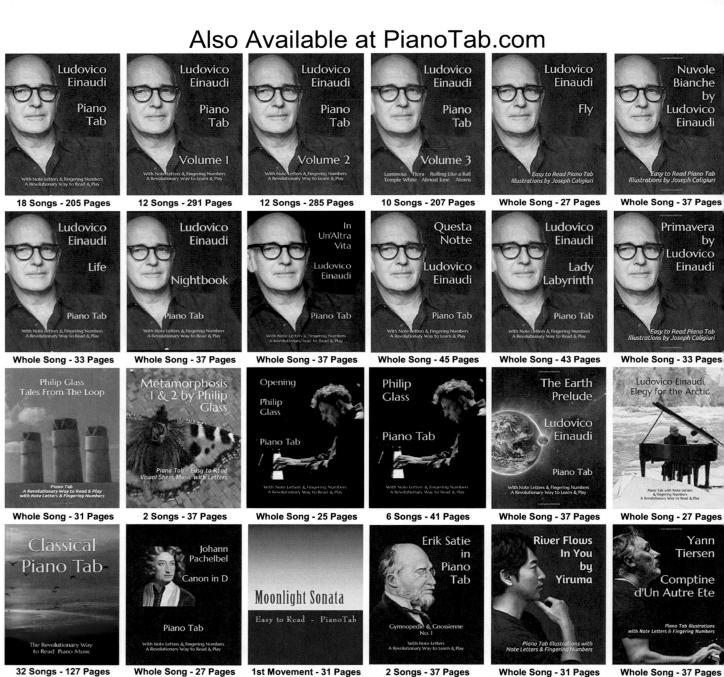

Ludovico Einaudi — Piano Tab	Ludovico Einaudi — Piano Tab — Volume 1	Ludovico Einaudi — Piano Tab — Volume 2	Ludovico Einaudi — Piano Tab — Volume 3	Ludovico Einaudi — Fly	Nuvole Bianche by Ludovico Einaudi
18 Songs - 205 Pages	12 Songs - 291 Pages	12 Songs - 285 Pages	10 Songs - 207 Pages	Whole Song - 27 Pages	Whole Song - 37 Pages
Ludovico Einaudi — Life	Ludovico Einaudi — Nightbook	In Un'Altra Vita — Ludovico Einaudi	Questa Notte — Ludovico Einaudi	Ludovico Einaudi — Lady Labyrinth	Primavera by Ludovico Einaudi
Whole Song - 33 Pages	Whole Song - 37 Pages	Whole Song - 37 Pages	Whole Song - 45 Pages	Whole Song - 43 Pages	Whole Song - 33 Pages
Philip Glass — Tales From The Loop	Metamorphosis 1 & 2 by Philip Glass	Opening — Philip Glass	Philip Glass — Piano Tab	The Earth Prelude — Ludovico Einaudi	Ludovico Einaudi — Elegy for the Arctic
Whole Song - 31 Pages	2 Songs - 37 Pages	Whole Song - 25 Pages	6 Songs - 41 Pages	Whole Song - 37 Pages	Whole Song - 27 Pages
Classical Piano Tab	Johann Pachelbel — Canon in D	Moonlight Sonata	Erik Satie in Piano Tab	River Flows In You by Yiruma	Yann Tiersen — Comptine d'Un Autre Ete
32 Songs - 127 Pages	Whole Song - 27 Pages	1st Movement - 31 Pages	2 Songs - 37 Pages	Whole Song - 31 Pages	Whole Song - 37 Pages
Beethoven in Tablature	Für Elise in Piano Tab	Mozart in Tablature	Passacaglia — George Frederick Handel	Prelude in C Major — Bach in Piano Tab	Bach — Prelude in B Minor
5 Songs - 33 Pages	Whole Song - 35 Pages	7 Songs - 28 Pages	Whole Song - 29 Pages	Whole Song - 25 Pages	Whole Song - 28 Pages
Snow — Fabrizio Paterlini	DNA — Ludovico Einaudi	Reverie — Ludovico Einaudi	Bach Piano Tab	Contemporary Piano	Two Trees — Ludovico Einaudi
Whole Song - 29 Pages	Whole Song - 33 Pages	Whole Song - 29 Pages	10 Songs - 39 Pages	26 Songs - 131 Pages	Whole Song - 35 Pages

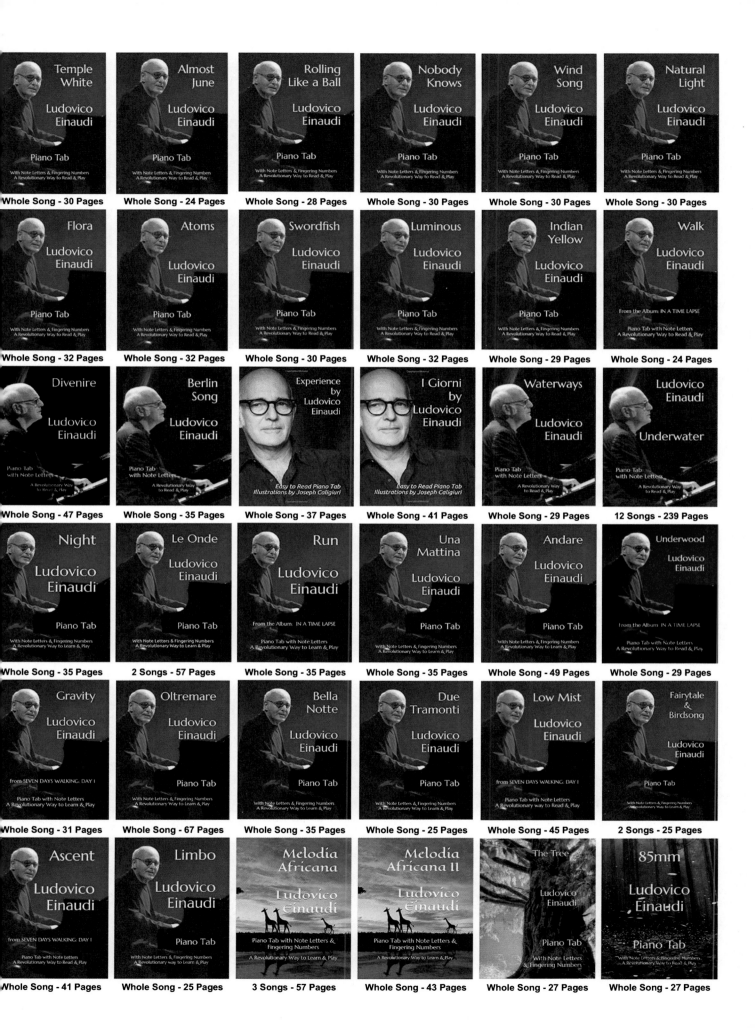

Temple White	Almost June	Rolling Like a Ball	Nobody Knows	Wind Song	Natural Light
Whole Song - 30 Pages	Whole Song - 24 Pages	Whole Song - 28 Pages	Whole Song - 30 Pages	Whole Song - 30 Pages	Whole Song - 30 Pages
Flora	Atoms	Swordfish	Luminous	Indian Yellow	Walk
Whole Song - 32 Pages	Whole Song - 32 Pages	Whole Song - 30 Pages	Whole Song - 32 Pages	Whole Song - 29 Pages	Whole Song - 24 Pages
Divenire	Berlin Song	Experience	I Giorni	Waterways	Underwater
Whole Song - 47 Pages	Whole Song - 35 Pages	Whole Song - 37 Pages	Whole Song - 41 Pages	Whole Song - 29 Pages	12 Songs - 239 Pages
Night	Le Onde	Run	Una Mattina	Andare	Underwood
Whole Song - 35 Pages	2 Songs - 57 Pages	Whole Song - 35 Pages	Whole Song - 35 Pages	Whole Song - 49 Pages	Whole Song - 29 Pages
Gravity	Oltremare	Bella Notte	Due Tramonti	Low Mist	Fairytale & Birdsong
Whole Song - 31 Pages	Whole Song - 67 Pages	Whole Song - 35 Pages	Whole Song - 25 Pages	Whole Song - 45 Pages	2 Songs - 25 Pages
Ascent	Limbo	Melodia Africana	Melodia Africana II	The Tree	85mm
Whole Song - 41 Pages	Whole Song - 25 Pages	3 Songs - 57 Pages	Whole Song - 43 Pages	Whole Song - 27 Pages	Whole Song - 27 Pages

Also Available at PianoTab.com

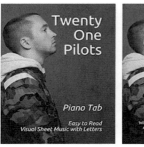

21 Songs - 76 Pages

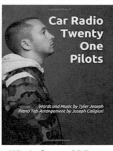

24 Songs - 101 Pages

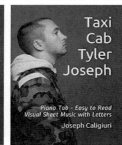

Whole Song - 25 Pages

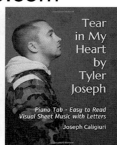

Whole Song - 25 Pages

Tear in My Heart by Tyler Joseph

Whole Song - 25 Pages

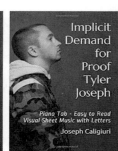

Whole Song - 29 Pages

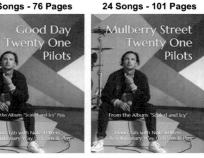

Good Day Twenty One Pilots

Whole Song - 25 Pages

Mulberry Street Twenty One Pilots

Whole Song - 29 Pages

Shy Away Twenty One Pilots

Whole Song - 27 Pages

Level of Concern by Twenty One Pilots in Piano Tab

Whole Song - 29 Pages

Hallelujah Leonard Cohen

Whole Song - 53 Pages

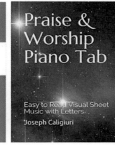

Clair de Lune by Claude Debussy

Whole Song - 27 Pages

How to Read **Piano Tab** — Play Piano by Letters

Method Book with over 50 Songs — Joseph Caligiuri

50 Songs - 77 Pages

Piano Tab Level 1 Lesson Book — Play Piano by Letters

15 Songs with Note Letters & Fingering Numbers — Joseph Caligiuri

15 Songs - 47 Pages

Piano Tab Level 2 Lesson Book — Play Piano by Letters

24 Songs with Note Letters & Fingering Numbers — Joseph Caligiuri

24 Songs - 81 Pages

Piano Tab Level 3 Lesson Book — Play Piano by Letters

25 Songs with Note Letters & Fingering Numbers — Joseph Caligiuri

25 Songs - 101 Pages

Piano Tab Level 4 Lesson Book — Play Piano by Letters

featuring songs by **Twenty One Pilots** — Joseph Caligiuri

24 Songs - 201 Pages

Praise & Worship Piano Tab

Easy to Read Visual Sheet Music with Letters — Joseph Caligiuri

19 Songs - 63 Pages

Life Blood — Fabrizio Paterlini

Whole Song - 33 Pages

Wind Song — Fabrizio Paterlini

Whole Song - 25 Pages

Week #6 — Fabrizio Paterlini

Whole Song - 25 Pages

Week #8 — Fabrizio Paterlini

Whole Song - 37 Pages

Day #2 My Misty Mornings — Fabrizio Paterlini

Whole Song - 31 Pages

Rue des Trois Frères — Fabrizio Paterlini

Whole Song - 25 Pages

Chandelier by Sia

Whole Song - 31 Pages

Movie & TV Theme Songs — Easy to Read Visual Sheet Music with Letters — Joseph Caligiuri

42 Songs - 131 Pages

Disney Collection — Easy to Read Visual Sheet Music with Letters "A Revolutionary Way to Read and Play Piano" — Joseph Caligiuri

24 Songs 77 Pages

Lionel Richie Piano Tab

5 Songs - 75 Pages

Monday Tom Odell Piano Tab

Whole Song - 35 Pages

My Heart Will Go On Celine Dion

Whole Song - 25 Pages

Piano Tab — Dust in the Wind — Kerry Livgren

Whole Song - 31 Pages

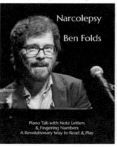

Call Me Blondie — Piano Tab

Whole Song - 41 Pages

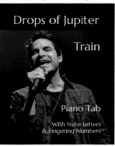

Narcolepsy Ben Folds

Whole Song - 29 Pages

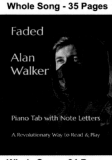

Drops of Jupiter Train Piano Tab

Whole Song - 33 Pages

Faded Alan Walker

Whole Song - 31 Pages

Barbie Girl - Aqua

Piano Tab with Note Letters

Whole Song - 35 Pages

200 Songs - 293 Pages	15 Songs - 101 Pages	30 Songs - 125 Pages	7 Songs - 81 Pages	Whole Song - 30 Pages	Whole Song - 37 Pages
Whole Song - 31 Pages	Whole Song - 31 Pages	Whole Song - 27 Pages	28 Songs - 79 Pages	Whole Song - 25 Pages	10 Songs - 35 Pages
Whole Song - 35 Pages	Whole Song - 25 Pages	Whole Song - 27 Pages	6 Songs - 79 Pages	Whole Song - 29 Pages	Whole Song - 39 Pages
Whole Song - 25 Pages	Whole Song - 27 Pages	Whole Song - 29 Pages	Whole Song - 27 Pages	Whole Song - 29 Pages	Whole Song - 31 Pages
Whole Song - 35 Pages	Whole Song - 35 Pages	Whole Song - 27 Pages	Whole Song - 27 Pages	Whole Song - 35 Pages	Whole Song - 31 Pages
Whole Song - 43 Pages	Whole Song - 27 Pages	Whole Song - 31 Pages	Whole Song - 35 Pages	25 Songs - 69 Pages	40 Songs - 54 Pages

Made in the USA
Las Vegas, NV
02 April 2024

88154339R00019